The Wise Men and Their Journey

YO-AWG-269

Illustrated by Gordon Stowell

WARNER PRESS, INC.
Anderson, Indiana

In the east there lived some wise men who studied God's wonderful creation. They were specially interested in the stars. They made big charts and maps showing the different groups of stars and how they moved around the sky.

One night they came across a star that they
had not seen before. They checked with
their maps and found that it was a new star.

The wise men read their books. "I think it means that a very special king has been born," said one wise man.
"We'll go and find out," they all agreed.

They called for their servants and told them to prepare for the journey.

"We must take presents as well, for the new king," they said.

Off they set. It was to be a long journey but
they were very excited about it. They
rested during the day from the hot sun,
and as they traveled at night, they found
that the new star seemed to be guiding
them.

Over hills and mountains the star led them.
It led them through valleys and across
rivers. They rode through forests, and they
crossed wide and dry deserts.

There were times when they were so tired
that they felt like giving up and going
home. But the star seemed to encourage
them, and gave them new energy to carry
on.

Soon they felt they were coming to the end of their journey. They arrived in Jerusalem. "Where is the new baby king of the Jews?" they asked.

The King of Judea, Herod, heard about the wise men. He sent for his advisors and asked them about the king of the Jews. They told him that he was to be born in Bethlehem. King Herod was worried.

King Herod sent for the wise men. "Go and look for this baby in Bethlehem," he said. "Let me know when you find him so that I can go and worship him, too." But secretly, King Herod planned to kill the baby.

The wise men continued their journey.
The star led them to the house where the
young child was.

Inside the house were Mary, Joseph and the young child, Jesus. This was the child that the wise men had traveled so far to see. This was the child who was born king of the Jews, the child who would be the Savior of the world.

The wise men entered. They knelt in front of Jesus and gave him the presents they had brought – gold, frankincense, and myrrh. The star had led them to their king.

They did not tell Herod where Jesus was.
They left Bethlehem and returned to their
own country by a different way.

The Christmas story can be found in
Matthew chapters 1 and 2.